Aliveness Is Always Young And Painted Almost Whole

Poetry

Lydia Cooley

BookLeaf Publishing

India | USA | UK

Copyright © Lydia Cooley
All Rights Reserved.

This book has been self-published with all reasonable efforts taken to make the material error-free by the author. No part of this book shall be used, reproduced in any manner whatsoever without written permission from the author, except in the case of brief quotations embodied in critical articles and reviews.

The Author of this book is solely responsible and liable for its content including but not limited to the views, representations, descriptions, statements, information, opinions, and references ["Content"]. The Content of this book shall not constitute or be construed or deemed to reflect the opinion or expression of the Publisher or Editor. Neither the Publisher nor Editor endorse or approve the Content of this book or guarantee the reliability, accuracy, or completeness of the Content published herein and do not make any representations or warranties of any kind, express or implied, including but not limited to the implied warranties of merchantability, fitness for a particular purpose.

The Publisher and Editor shall not be liable whatsoever...

Made with ❤ on the BookLeaf Publishing Platform
www.bookleafpub.in
www.bookleafpub.com

Dedication

To The Way of things

Preface

I bare this heart to you earnestly
I am beginning to you like a shadow *truly* begins
anciently
at the birth of the sun
When the shadow comes to you it shows itself
only as the instant babe of a young tree...
the shadow seems simple
yet the source, the creator of the shadow, the beingness
beside the reflection
is complex and forever

What speaks to you here begins anciently at the birth of
the sun
And here
you, and I, and It
can only be relating shadows
trickling into one sometimes
when the wind combs through the canopies

Creation is natural
so this book is like a stream
May this bring the reader
goodness and aliveness

With Love

-Lydia

Acknowledgements

I thank the world

A Love Letter Well Received

I think I feel you still
hovering around me
My skin has been fresh this day
coated in whispers that you left to run
like tiny children's tulip feet on my being
I saw 64 white roses in the shell
of a tired eye
Then a temple built of prayers;
they turned solid in their passing
and grew vines of mahogany and ginger
Then I felt the eve turn brown and saw
You
Looking into the sand
You say you see gold unfolding like an erotic sun
in the palm of a volcano
Then you see it
in your own palm
The sky is silent
I've never seen you before
But I once looked into a wall of darkness
and felt the same cheek smile under my lips
as I do on you,
as if it were my own face upside down
We lock eyes then you

don't speak at all

Oh how aroundness grew naked

Not a whimper from any hole or spot or orbit

I can only suppose we found the exact

In between of everything

Where existence desires,

in one glimpse,

to exist

My poetics about this will go on

for my whole life

I will never line lines up

to replicate the way the universe was

when us together

was created

We are separate yes, like light and dark

Then made as one in another place

As shadow

You see?

The goshawk let out a cry

The red tail, a cry

I, a cry

You, a cry

We are noble and unclean and rambling prophets

walking the fine line of a poet that goes seeking meeting

the teacher who meets the medium in the sky in the eye

who talks to our lost and loves the pathways and

remembers Gypsies who sing songs and dance for their

lovers and they remember the writers that struck them
with their ponderous curiosity and surrenderant
position
You are the man of my encompassing
because right now I am all encapsulated
My straining organs that love you now
they'll loosen their lust but will not forget
The holy certainty I feel about loving you
Makes me wonder who I am again
Am I not just
a simple beast
charged with a life
full of signals and transmissions?
Poised to become awareness
then be human again
like a little play on words
like chorus to bridge
Like your morning singing to me
Like your mourning to me
Your innocent sleep
You are like the perfect waking stretch and also
the most desolate echoing cry
My dawns will always know you
I'll grey and you'll put flowers in my hair
You'll grey and I'll put flowers in your hair
We'll grey and hold our breath in the ocean
and dance to each others drums

May your nowness be utterly lovely
Peaceful
Divine
I love you
I'll find more ways to say it
It's on my tongue like
a gasp for sobbing air
I am sobbing inside as I write this
I hope to cry
I feel it coming
I'm almost there
I'm coming
I'm crying
You are my orgasm and
my guttural weeping
I love you
I love you
Good night
Grand rising
With sweetness,
Your love,
Lydia.

Speaking With the Monk

There was never a farewell
Between the offspring of the egg and its shell
Never a wince
Between the shadow of dusk
And the antique railroads final moan
I spoke with a friend who has since
Lessened his becoming
After we made love
Furthered his namelessness
As instant as the point of a needle now
No tracing where I've been pricked
No wound to heal just a nerve that's been touched

Now time is fasted to our elusive mouths
He is a helpless nimble forest of kelp
Dancing the inner ocean's hand-me-down melody

Through the telephone the monk and I
Had words leaking from our conscious swells
The absolute of our entire lives can be found
Reflected in his motions
Expecting none receiving none pure being is his passion
Undone from lust
A ripple caught on a lilting wind

I lay in white soon
Bided by undercurrent wind
It's red maple leaves
Black noses of shade
White feathers
My head on the black pillow on the white bed
The diety stoned me in my figurative sleep
Applying fleshless concaves to the folds of the brain
Like the holy rapture would walk on strips of plastic to
reach the Undoable human
They decided me as their object again
When I couldn't hold
My body laid me on its side
I could sense the galaxy's mind like the fumes from a
penis tip
When he is about to cum
The muscular revolve of this light enraptured me
to obey
Like a woman in need of guidance
Not like a
Trapped child

It told me
"You are the number"

Then a dog barked and scratched on the door

Anubis

Gone when I woke

Not A Thing Of It

Sweat on the tip of the tongue of the unspoken
Mouth hollow whining
Holes poked into the nothing
I want to see in color and speak in black or in white
Trudging through metaphor
Like I am the will of the inanimate
The twists and turns of grasses arouse all that
I will never say
Not a thing of it
This is why I kiss necks and pick my finger wounds

You and Summer and An Uphill Dream

I would hear the frost tickle the belt of summertime
with its ember fingertip
I used my entire life in those moments
We were blanched in the canyons consecrated memory
Burning sun on the soft boyish willow as it nakeds itself
Where the children of our soul undress for bath

A scorpion small enough to nip me a few times
Wrothe me, I became the haven of a thing that is used, a
thing which's death means most to its life
Then I had the journey
Up the hill into the forest land
Mother listens and laughs
I drive the lonely cycle up a slippery hill

Hermit

the mind is
like a hermit
like a dog flowers head
like some stranger
like a portrait of a lady dead
like a hoodlum in a song
singing masochistic licks
like an artist in a bedsheet
covered in crumbs and candle lit

Belonging

I wove into the gentle blue waking of a morning
after a week
A Sunday winter fog after a satisfying flush of night
I took note of becomings
Of different ways I could direct the mode of self
A fruit on a limb
Juiced by sun and rain
But as I lay next to you
The solid rock cool in the cave
A soft teather tucked me back down
As a young anemone
bid to rest under a long tidal exhale
My chest cavity blightless
I belonged to love
In a new way
I honored it more than
The cursive hand writes and prophetic breakfast pursuits
and the cuffed wrist of coffee shaking my glowing hand
Finally my youth and my age were letting minnows
swim through their separation
My elder self holds me first born
And I adore towards
the imperfect freckles on your back

Begin With Her Word and Go On

Over tiss tossed hiss lands
Riddled to keep suckers searching for snakes and
dried rice
Cactus-like-clouds kiss the rain and freckle it sharply
Turnt over ideas of lost genius
Swallowed by too much mind
Not enough rice
Galewood wraps around fat feet
Constituates mold along these flat lands
Still crooked
Crooked by nook piles of nettles and one lost eyeball
Believe that
This eyeball: the only substance of its likeness
Other than a newt
So it drew to it, dust
And metal-molecule
The Mercury of this river caused fish to eat the matter
Then the iris sank
It was found to be heavy
Quite heavy
Alike to silver but invisible like water
What a stupid comparison
I am obviously vacant at the cortex of my mind

In regard to ideas

    A simple word, A complex channel

Between

I am sitting between my entire life
Two green benches are my entirety
Sky and bird call make up my mind
I go as they go
I am writing here...words...yes.
thoughts, as I check,
are slim petals, I go to describe and they grow thicker
with pollen.
The deepest me is very far into the goopy well of this.
Goodness I've gone on explaining it for a while, I love to
dance, it feels good to speak.
What an impeccable mutation of biology and spirit;
reasonable and still fluky.
The word "AND" is so important to me.
How important can words be?
I might be done because I've unspun and am kindling a
fire just with the sight of these two benches that can be
blue if I look and green if I look!
I had a dream of a dismembered woman and it was
spiritual. She was tossing herself around, going mad like,
"get it off me!" "I'm done and ready to be none!"
An excited pressure like mania.
I suppose she symbolizes this whole toss up going on as
part of my evolution

Aha, I see myself as one blip in forever again, why do I go on then??????

Because I am not so simple and I bond my troubles with the sky in its inability to touch the ground...I might be foolish for that one...but it doesn't mind my metaphor. The sky is very very very blue! Makes the tables look green again.

Ah, there goes the train, it's got a featureless face I see when I hear it's horn go, distant mother calling on supper, but I am way out in the green hay fields.

My brother is by the wharf collecting golden wrappers. We will not be home until much later and we will have to run so far to catch the last push of the setting sun, so she calls now, 11:00am, to give us time.

The truth is I do not know where my brother is, but I know he is safe. I heard his child voice in my head for the first time since that was his only voice, it was sweet oh my god it was sweet.

His current laugh which is deeper than our fathers
is special and unsettlingly new.

I miss him.

Oh dear.

Is that wrong?

I miss who he used to be because

He was the one child I knew.

Really knew.

The way I knew me.

Now he is a man I must understand again.
A stranger born from the blood of my heart
And reflection grows cold between two beholders that
separate into smoke and soot.
I look longingly and without any thought that wouldn't
belong to the desperate call of a fog horn, "Look at me"
Calling for my brother in thin air.
Do you feel me? Is it that easy?
We can't know. We might be shown, little
By little
Little little children
Growing all grown up
I've got a big long dress on that hugs me like a woman
Goddamn me!
I am a woman!
This is why I keep my eyes ever neutral and ongoing.
Grow grow grow
Death!
What a fine master, life designed as the teaching.
Genius you are, Death.
Without you, what would this be?
What this would be!
Oh dear it would be scary without you.
Oh dear it would be...just like it was before...I don't want
to go back yet...not yet...not just yet...

Goodbye for now, the day exists so much!

I wish I could kiss you, comprehender
But you're like my elbow
I'll see you in thin air
I'll be you in thin air
Thank you,
God Heart to the heavens, I thank YOU!

Lover Like Bird

Summer Lover
You were like a patterned cradle into the sunset
Like a river rock smiling up at me
Uneeding peaceful thing
You were always sort of like a jar
Full of mostly light
And just a few fireflies

The lover of January was a dying fetus in the
spring garden
He taught me impeccable word
Careful with my thought
Generous with my tongue
He reminded me that the true meaning always shows
readable on my face
Diligence is an absolute
Stillness must be extreme

October brought the poise of a blue jay
Cracking a whip at my side
Coloring a white room
Easy intention
The integrity of flame
Wavering whilst eternal

Procedure of Usefullness

I am very tired and
need to be associated with something
A damned piano plays until untuned
then the playing isn't up to it any longer
nor the user
as he becomes a mute beholder
who is just
a dire skin
in the procedure of usefulness
and the beauty installed for purpose
and long wet nasty decay of the
unidentifiably alive

We Become Cast to Acquiescence

A clearaway shovel picks at a buildup of years
Puckered up at the base of a thick pine
The flat rain hangs in the balance
Untying the cradle from its wrist
A stream upheaves a new buckle in its knee

The morning is paused under the bill of a magpie
Daphnia consume its salvations
All at once the town wakes and it
pauses the clouds
The unused pink mansion became chalked in flame
Like true stone it stood with a toned pec
I adored at that shapeful moment of elder ember
The apparition of no one

Then we prowl our egos at its symbolism
like humans eat fruits for plump sex and cheese for fine
status and wine for deep thought and nuts for will and
strength
We become cast to acquiescence
like pans in the backyard
Ambulances gibe at us
swallowing our smallness

Our lives a cubist paintwork
Who paints us subsist in the
micro detailed orientation
of flesh's script
It takes an inception to believe in the self again
Not even leaves as yellow as the magpies bill will cast
brimful belief as my way
Not even the neon lizard will snap me as alive as
The daffodils
I put one in my hair as a prissy child
Seeing each other is a trampoline
"Nice to see you"
We are alive and you are also in
Colorful scarves and compressed woolen arms
Then you go and a whiff of everafter gathers itself as a
blasé mannequin in my brain
The brain pulsates and melts into
the self
Finally again I am safe from identification

After A Conversation

Earrings over ice us
Bare to barren faces
Contraction bellies
Bound in and then flail
Discomfort turns beige like a reflection
Cold death and erect stems
Sickness is a buoyant feeling
Smells of natural toxics ungulate
Sex on the rim of eyes popping out
Imagining gore and butterfly tongues

Crooks

I crook in to fit
the tiny warm light uninterrupted by building
Cold in the same ways I am unsure
I fit into this corner with small children
They shouldn't yet need to know
But I am older
and I should know
I think I had a dream of aging
My skin and mind more folds
Would you rather be warm
or be cold and feel sunlight?
Are our rathers relevant?
Now I'm back it's days later and it's late evening
Dark
On the same roof
Wind and wet and
Now I am sure
Still liminal
Still almost at the edge
But sure
Am what I am what this is
Until I die
Then finally I go
It can rest awhile in the purple

Before returning
Crooking in to fit

Fragile

25

I feel as fragile
as glass
knowing itself
the moment before
free falling

If I Were a Train Somehow

If I were a train somehow
or swung myself through a rolling machine
or sharpened my laziness on a can
or bought out some of the ocean and stuck it to my teeth
or got drunk off a wire and hung like a bat
or struck dead
but only the outermost of my skin
or if I was too tired to sleep or had too many faces stuck
on me to dream
or if I was waning in on sunshine and wore out my boots
doing it
or if I was the coin of a guitar
or if my hands didn't cramp
or if I were a porch pillow, a hat, or a madman's scarf
worn as a belt
or if i kept writing two years past the click
or if I resembled nothing at all
and somehow not even humanhood
or if I were a cat on coffee or a crack rock stuck in a foot
or a pencil with bullets made of lead
or a flying piece of metal like a led zeppelin or a bullet
If I were a wound
I would be a humungous lethal hole caught in the jungle
right in the middle of the chest

If I were a lawn, I would also be the tick in it
If I thought, I'd still say nonsensical things like
black blue equals grey butter
and mean it too
And If that was the last set of words in my head before
death
I would revel like a sailor crisply smelling the jasmine of
the shore
I would revolve like the onward nature of being alive
I would be the nature of reguardlessness
I would bike along the rim of a shadow
and know breaths that jump straight out of the heart
I almost accidentally stopped my heart by thinking about
it strangely
If I were a twirl I would not stop but I would drop in
rivers for delight
If I would,
then I have, I will, I must, or I am
So to be anything
I have to be this right now

A Young Shape

Patience
Like a melody
Unsilken from the bounty of tomorrow
I love your distant hands
When they mean everything to the music and
Nothing to my skin
I love you more before we try into each other
As we divine our depths
through the dim pink reflections in the dark barroom
Why I love you is your tough and floral fingertips
You are honest yet strategic
God will you just sex me like you do that guitar
Forget me just play me
An instrument of your divinest soul
Crunch your heart upon my bleeding everything
I belong to the lily field and its moonlight
Be my seed spreading wind
I am a gem of your shadow
and you
a star
flickering just in my eye
I'll dance my revolving breath into your black curls
A young shape we are

Where the Wrens and Swallows Weave the Day

Dance and the heart will follow
I leap through the moonlight reminiscences
of the laughing child-land
at daybreak
The saturated brush of birds
explode into being
sweeping their violet crosshatched paths
swift like the paperboy
quiet and chirpy
Rising to the backscatter of rose gold
The remainder of this
shutters like a newly framed window
Adjusting itself on the braces of winter
I dull in midair as an acorn
Unnoticed freedom ticks like swelling wood
Gone in the passerby's wink
Just house paint, house rocks, and frozen wind

Only a moment...
Before the entire fire of my heart
reminded the middle eye
To still in such preserved warmth
The discomfort relaxed upon me

All remains as it is in silence
All remains as it resides beside your life

The residue drops a calming ripple upon the breast of a
mid ocean wave
I bevel into the spiraling
for licks and lyric that free my body
Of any ailment who fooled me in disguise
Nothing belonged to me but
I belonged in the mutant delicacy
Hung as a lonely tree branch
Given a scratch by the wind
As thankful as one who is humble

Sensitive space sometimes smells rotten
Sometimes a poppy's soul is the most fragrant
Take no offense to those sensitive to opium
The truth is heaven
The truth is the movement of angels
The guardianship of water
Where there is drought someday
There will be rain
Maybe inside of the makeup of the sun is
A water so nourishing
It would bring us back
From instant ash

All spirit is instant and forever
The morning never faded
I never moved
The hundred toed tap dance of the
yellow breast starlings
and the
dusty wren
and those
rowdy jays
and
lilty blue birds
On the roses of the church
and the
steps of the oaks
and
beside the neighborhood sixty foot ginkgo
and at the
tip of the old palm
All shifted into the bust of emergent cold
empty air
Purple and red and yellow just alike
But open mouthed
One caravel up on the shifty sea-way
Exploring its gulfs in earnest compassion
With wind
Tosses us unto above-ness
Dive and die then alive in laughter

Little dancer within her
The child has always been the master
Loved one
Loved ones
No one forsaken
A wonderful life
Nothing given nothing taken
Is-ness for all
Wading in
Low and mighty
Through high tide

To Get to the Stars with a Story

After I posed my entirety into womanly tears
A bucket of endearing madness
We dulled as if infatuation is a falsetto that gets higher
until no one can hear but
The quiet hound in the brick house
Who perks like we do when we hear a bell
A draft of thought
An angel is getting its wings
Or a love is ascending
I couldn't even tell if I was being honest
But I used my every sense to figure it out
I was too close to the mirror
Could only eat my words
His eyes blackened at me as if I...
Now here is where I don't want to
draw conclusions on another...it's
Too hard to see through
But it seems
He can't fall into my void
I become so unreal
Like a dissociated train pass
Then I speak of the train and no one can
Ever think of me sane

I saw what didn't happen
That is internal life
And so he reposes all he knows
Between our wit and how he
Should hold a woman
And he woman's me
And I'm his woman
And I'm a little girl
But I can only feel myself as void
And so it doesn't work
Then he looks empty to me
Where is your boyness?
Won't you cry?
Then I spite myself for wishing majesty into a growing
sky
I am like a haunted mother

This morning I wake and think of all the
The impeccable reaches I am
Indifferent to
I think of being carful with my words
I think of ceremony
I think of nerve
And of running
To and away
I wonder
Am I a bug on a wire

that is the web of a spider?
Am I the inside of a fruit
fallen to the floor
Goop but alive and
No wonder I am confused then
I searched for the crack in our understanding and peeled
it
I want canyon after canyon
Amaze me or go
Like I'm some empty plot only accepting
Masterpiece skies
But the land I reference is deferential
Accepts all
vacancies and despondencies above
Accepts the foot stomping blaze
Even trills a happy story from it
Even gifts chamomile to her torturers
She acts meek because she is all mighty
And maybe that is why I let him
I want to nurture the boy and befriend the guy and
absorb the wisdom of the man
But I tread carefully as to not utilize him
Like sailboats utilize wind
He wouldn't like that
But then I ask
What do you use me for?
If you don't want to dip eternally into

My non-beingness
Do you not only want to enrapture the curves of my
shape and consume the divinity there-within?
Are we incapable of not using each other
Selfishly?
I ask truly
How long does it take to achieve
Perfect balance
Needless exchange
Proper transaction
We all have one goal
Get to the stars with a story
A story that echoes
Like a song like
Like everything echoes
It's not about
Yes or no
Or how
I'm sorry young one
Cry and cry and
Clamp your heart again
Then release the blood
You will find solace
Along the way

Insight Day

Today the morning sparrows do
dovestance in the rain
Melt and pull and lapse a refrain
above like a nonchalant past of a man
who uses other people's fate
A fallout of heaven has come down
Measuring the temperance of waking
I am a white moth on a cill
So I see the imagination of everything

I ask the bricks if I am doing right
They laugh in their collected puddle
I see the rust reflection of my deepest symphony
I die easy then reborn in the moment there
Thank you ruby rocks
For playing each string of my heart
With each pebble in your skin

Save a space
Near by the beach of the swamp
Near your artery
Cry there and be brushed back and around
by stalky winds
Dream of strange vegetable collecting

Ease for retrieving
Need for accessing
A hunger that is debatable
Faces on the lamp and the voice
that joins me just before sleep
Stillness
Continues
One place
In a winter
Thankful grace
Excitable responses
Those humans of our kind
Our lives
who know us
who were affected by us
They carry on
and I only know this
Small cup of coffee

Troubled Idea In an Open Day

Paled idea of noon
But it is night
Now stars are straw and fall all cracked
Disturbing the defeated grass

Crickets fail to breath
Dehydrating the sonic belt that is about to
Convey dawn
Now the morning opens its eyes
Stares stiff through broken window blinds
Into a pinkly bruised sky
The gasping is mute and droolless
The metaphor of sun and gun write
Pages worth about themselves
Onto the shredded blanks
Redundant like paisley
A rapid remark sits beside the air and
Plays me
Because I am a blue utterance worth
Nothing
Stuck in long dark dells of listening
I haven't even woken my body yet and
I am met with this heft!

The first sip of the day is a crack in time
Only misery will follow its hollow sanctity!
I want to go back into sleeping

Sturdy wet stems are my violet veins
Thin and stalwart as ant legs
They are trains of gashed obsidian that
Contain themselves
Throughout the things
That are my eye's lids
They are like raw-cut-thin-sliced pork belly
That somehow bloomed a base
Of slimy chicken skin
My flaps are soft like a silken tattoo
And they cover up my forever open eyeballs
Desperately hiding the eternal wake
I forget and I rest
Death is the trademark of this life

I have now left bed
A woman matches the slow trot
Of breezes after midnight
Vital pigment in her distress
Vital pigment is her truth
Do you see how it is necessary?
The pigment?

Lovers are fickle when in
Loud when out
He told me about
Thin and opaque
He is little to none
Like the counted droplets of a wave
Which is why he points his face loudly at me
With such bountiful conviction
I am conscious this man is too a gentle one
But I am the fated outermost petal
Of a magnolia flower
Who will delicately fall to the ground
In a sweet setting of ambrosia
A naked woman exampling god to life
And life to god
The wretched betweens are my meat
I only have sex with the sun which leaves me
Moaning and moaning
My thin arms pulsing with muscle
Like a chestnut
And they relax into a neat ribbon bow
Then the celibate blossoms bud bud bud
Blow on the tight undoable ribbon bow
We'll need to cut the knot
To be fertile again
Those remnants of utter-truth
Are the epitome of nothing

Ha ha
I laugh at the designless nature of faces
They all light up in the sunlight!
Not a single one defies all odds
I want to see the shadow person
Steal the dames conception of day
She has been waiting! For reality to come
Bash her like an instant rain
She will be in little pain comparatively

Look at her feet!
They curl twists into flexible tendons
Red blue bones are peeling
Like the anxious grass blade
Will do in its politeness

She is finally just midday
No more the woman who walks streets
She is only now just simply a flatbed
Catching the blossoms that rot
After children bruise them

She feels like, if you can imagine, this:
An orgasm pumping through a corpses face
Who's Self left the body stunned
At the ravenousness of death

Painted quickly by nature
An image of spirit
Through way of petrifying stone
Then clarifying the body to an ash
That is soft diamond
Last leaving a tracer of a stoic
And merciful face
But you could not really see it
Not at all even if you had the eyes of god
This is why I explain her absence to you
In a metaphorical opacity
Feeling her is a comparative feeling to
Briefly thinking you've just seen
Your dead mother walk by
But it is absolute illusion
Working with the the jester of
After-casted memory
Sweet memory is so delicate and hopeful
Like a flags dingy pole
Like the hands of a claysmith

I focused in deep
To the morning activity
Of sculpting!
It is what I always do with this head and
These words
Beaten and battered up

A barren mind multiplying
Self by Self
Time times Time
I am tired between my eyes
I shut in quiet
Gray tea is cold now and can't prevent me
From dozing away

I have left the heat of my impulses
Stuffed behind the worn down factory
Of my previous self
I can only exist at the precipice of death
Though you'll still see me living

Young and Painted Almost Whole

Who of us chooses the time at which
We develop our breasts and joints and callouses...
Who of us has control of our
Artistic desires or passing wonders...
Who of us is completed?
I stand before myself in a manic wonder
Aweing at this being I admire and adore and
Do not really recognize
Why have I twisted myself into
A shape?
What happens when my inner waters change
And the sediment outside is crunchy and unchippable?
Will I erode like earth or give my self up? Up to where?
To be a mother I would retract my love for my own adolescence
I would forgo the will to better my "self"
And I would embrace the light of the one who was born
The one who I was born as
And then I would become the highest face within the meditation
The new child born as then
Would become the symbol of my best ability
Of my humanhood raw

So until that
Why do I paint myself
Shouldn't I forget this foolish tattoo and become mud?
Maybe if I only *look* through my eyes, not *think* of them
I forgo beauty and become the eye of beauty
The seeing and not the seen
Maybe I should be only
The something
I will rise into a dusty rose periwinkle only as a
Hue to be seen through
I'll be a birds sign wave
An instrument
Reconfigurable
Reconfigure
Love
Be Loved
Regardless
Be born on top of self
Again
Layer legs
Grow even more than more
Brace the self for not breaking
For being infinitely unbreakable
We are used to the illusion of
Breakage
I am an eternal tide I must stay awake
I must watch and stay as the wake

Conquering without defeat
Without war and battle
Rest
Justice is done in this place
Know thy tongue is responsible to dance what is
choreographed by the tongueless

Round I go as music!
Lust fall away!
I relieve you of this tangent!